Electromagnetic Field Computers and Robots

A New Type Of Machine

By Jamil Kazoun
(Jamil Talaat Malak Sukkarieh Kazoun)

Version 1

Forward

As of today, I am not aware of any other writings on the subject, the subject of creating a computer or a robot from purely electromagnetic fields, that is, not from solid state material. Just as a radio wave is a purely electromagnetic form, so can these computers and robots be made from. An electromagnetic field structure, that is practically weightless, inhabiting nearly any space and goes though it and through barriers, can change shape and size, and can use energy available in space or provided to it. A giant leap in speed, efficiency and abilities compared to even today's most advanced computers and robots, a quantum leap that can and likely will propel technology, and even humanity to a different level.

Jamil Kazoun

Dec 26, 2018

This book is mostly a very brief compilation taken from my other work, as it relates to electromagnetic computers and robots. It is an extremely short book, a booklet, meant simply to lay the foundation for this new area, for invention and design, that will create such machines. Just as the Maxwell's equations for the most part are few lines on a piece of paper and were the foundation for electrical engineering and the ensuing tools and machines that were created, I hope these few words will now serve to be the foundation and motivation for the new field of tools and machines to be created from electromagnetic fields and later possibly other non-solid state materials.

Not much attention is given to composition or other editorial and grammatical elements as I am barely able to dedicate my energy and focus as I wish. I can hardly work to type at the computer or manage my daily chores. Forgive my mistakes, of disorganization or paragraphs or grammatical or spelling errors if any. That is not important and is trivial in such a new work, and under the severe personal health struggle I face to be able to get the work out.

This book is inspired by my experience in the spirit world, were some beings seem to be made from completely electromagnetic field-like forms. Enter the field with humility, and without arrogance.

Jamil

Creating A Brand New Type Of Machines

The history of computing tools and machines is extremely recent. In the old age and history of mankind, nothing is recorded beyond few hundred years. In tens of thousands of years, there is nothing to be found. The abacus seemed to be the exception, few thousand years old, a very primitive mechanical computing tool, but so primitive that it can be discounted. Charles Babbage is reported to have worked on the first mechanical computers: at https://en.wikipedia.org/wiki/Charles_Babbage

It says " Charles Babbage ; 26 December 1791 – 18 October 1871) was an
English polymath. A mathematician, philosopher, inventor and mechanical engineer, Babbage originated the concept of a digital programmable computer.
Considered by some to be a "father of the computer", Babbage is credited with inventing the first mechanical computer that eventually led to more complex electronic designs, though all the essential ideas of modern computers are to be found in Babbage's analytical engine. His varied work in other fields has led him to be described as "pre-eminent" among the many polymaths of his century.
Parts of Babbage's incomplete mechanisms are on display in the Science Museum in London. In 1991, a functioning difference engine was constructed from Babbage's original plans. Built to tolerances achievable in the 19th century, the success of the finished engine indicated that Babbage's machine would have worked."

No matter, this history is very recent by human development age. And nearly only the last 70 years have seen the creation of electronic computers. The development path has taken an exponential growth path, leading to tremendous progress in the field in an extremely brief period, and the process has not stopped. Tools and machines of all sorts in the electronics and communication fields are available that are efficient and inexpensive, available to the public.

But now is the time to start on a more dramatic growth and radical path in the history of machine making. The path of building machines from electromagnetic fields. These machines will be far superior to current technology. In terms of machine computational speeds, efficiency, flexibility, form, cost, and nearly every aspect they are far superior. The problem with this new field, which can be called Electromagnetical Engineering, is that these are the founding ideas only. What will be needed is developing the understanding of what is needed for basic functional building blocks to develop these computers and robots from non-solid state electromagnetic fields, and to develop the needed mathematics and computer programing to aid in the design and manufacturing. Just as the vacuum tube, diode, and transistor, served in part as basic elements that helped lead to the creation of the new electronic computers and robots, this novel field will have similar needs. The field is basically starting from zero, and much work and creativity will be needed.

These novel new machines, will be weightless, superfast, flexible in design, can travel thru space and thru material, from water and oceans, to outer space and the planets in seconds or minutes, will be in size unimaginably small or unimaginably big, or can in an instant switch between sizes, and go inside the human body to look, fix or destroy unobtrusively. They will go to outer space to look and explore like we could never come close to doing now. The machines will resemble spirits in some ways, and will take us eventually towards that path in the future, for development, or communication, or life extension by transposing our memory into these robots, at will, for life extension or different life experiences, just as is the case for the current function of some spirits.

About me

As someone that studied mathematics and electrical engineering, and was involved in computer programing and artificial intelligence programing and research, it was my experience in the spirit realm that brought me into this subject completely unexpectedly. I believe these EMF machines I talk about will be the future of computing and robotics for a long time.

Research

The challenges for creating basic components or components from non-solid state electromagnetic material, such as electromagnetic fields, is that currently as far as I know, we do not know how to do it. Non-solid state electromagnetic fields in their different forms have no development for being the stand alone medium for computing. Current computers are based on silicon based solid state circuits, or different solid state materials. We know how to do this very well, and understand the technology, and have developed the tools. Billions of computations per second for a simple inexpensive computer are readily available based on such technologies. But we have no idea how to build the basic components in non solid state electromagnetic fields (EMF) materials. In silicon, a transistor is easily made, and a circuit with a million or a billion component of these intricately connected are possible. But using purely EM waves or fields material as a base, we do not know how to build any such basic components/functionality as far as I know. It needs to be invented. How to build a transistor, or a diode, or better maybe, a completely new basic component, that can be used to build more complex components from EMF, to build the new computers and robots from.

How do we learn to draw, paint and sculpture freely in the three dimensional world using EM fields, electromagnetic waves, on a CAD/CAM with functionality in mind? We can start from basic EMF equations, and numerical and finite element computer programing of these equations. We can use random generation to help in the exploration for finding traditional or novel solutions. But sometimes, in a new field, it may be best to look afresh at the issues of computing for a basic unit such as a transistor, and to move beyond the traditional structures we know to something more suitable for the new material and its nature. But being clueless, we can start by evolution, of trying to emulate current methodology in design, and look at novel new ways suitable for the new medium when creativity comes.

Example new machines (computers and robots):
1. Free standing computers in space. Invisible. Weightless. Can perform special functions. One or thousands or billions of them can be in the space of a room. More advanced are when they have communication abilities and will work together on a task in parallel or adaptive topology suitable for the task.
2. Robotic machine. Can do robotic tasks by motion. Others have sensors. Others have computation ability (computer).
3. Robots with a structure that allows penetration of different materials, such as penetrating water, solid materials such as walls, and human body, etc. Inside the human body they can go in and out, see, fix, or destroy. As they can do in other spaces.
4. Robots of different sizes, from nano and pico meters and much further beyond in being small, to kilometers and thousands of kilometers big, on the other side of the scale. Other robots, can change size, and shape adaptively in discrete steps or

fluidly while maintaining functionality in full or partially to suit requirements. They will travel to planets in minutes, explore, share experience, and perform tasks.

5. Billions can be generated efficiently, in seconds or minutes, to allow different types of computing and robotics platforms and functionalities. Spread in space unobtrusively, at almost any point, with minimal energy requirements.

6. The challenge of energy supply for these machines needs to be solved. Initially, it is possible as one option to have solid state energy sources available till better options are available. A computer or robot can use a battery or electric line to tap into as an energy source. Even a car engine or any rotating object nearby can be used for that purpose. The computers and robots even though can tap to a solid state battery, they are not attached to it, but can do so, by moving part of its body to touch the battery as needed, to attach or detach. Of course, it seems best to use energy sources from the same medium these machines are made of. Energy in space is abundant in space for these machines, from photons in the entire spectrum, to other possible sources. Recently, wireless energy transfer has become available commercially in forms of induction energy, which can supply such machines in limited ways.

Start The Brain Storming Process

A simple EM wave can be a sine wave. It has the nature of moving forward in space. We need to be able to force such waves, or other forms of waves or surfaces or structures to be self-constrained in space, bounded by a physical and controllable location. Starting with one or two dimensions may not give such ability. Looking into three dimensions, we may start to imagine ways of producing such structures that use the electric field and magnetic fields in them to achieve these requirements. So we may need to start from a high point of complexity at a minimum. I imagine for example a wave being produced along a spherical surface path instead of a traditional linear path, as would an electron orbit an atom or an energy field. We need to start at the beginning phases of generation of the EM waves, in order to understand all that can be done at this point to explore the possibilities. Starting from some analogies, in the atomic world, where a particle may have tendency to continue in a straight line, but other forces trap it in an orbit or space, or better to use the internal dynamics and structures of the EM field (the electric and magnetic components of the field) as the trapping and control mechanism. I throw out these ideas without too much thought simply in order to kick start the brain storming process, even if unfruitful. What is important is to start! Start meetings, discussions, illustrations, spreading the word and ideas in order to get the process of new development going. And also when something is novel, sometimes it helps to go back to the basics and foundations of the science involved.

EMF Machines: From EM waves and fields as carriers of information, to becoming a processor of it, and the structure of the processor.

Millions and millions of electromagnetic waves may touch you or go inside your body every moment. Do you see them? Do you feel them? But if you placed a radio next to you, then you can detect some of them, in some frequency ranges, and listen to what they are carrying in sound information, so-to-speak. So you listen to the radio. The radio signal is electromagnetic, and is near you, and is also touching your skin and body, and is also going inside your body, and part of it is going thru your body. So millions of electromagnetic waves carrying information are constantly touching your body and going inside it. Similarly for tv waves, carrying sound and images and moving images touch your body and go inside it.

Remember or do you know that maybe only fifty years ago, a vacuum tube or solid-state transistor was the size of your finger, and now it is so small, you cannot see it with the naked eye, and millions of it can fit on your finger? That is what a modern computer chip is made from. Now, can you imagine a transistor made from an electromagnetic material, as an electromagnetic field or waves? Just like we make radio and TV signals from electromagnetic wave material. This structure can move in space, carry information AND PROCESS information! It is invisible, super-fast in travel, will enter your body, and can touch your skin, and the skin of all the people in your city, or your country, and earth if need be if the signal is strong enough. So what is a computer made on a single silicon chip? Many transistors linked together to store and process information. Well, instead of a single electromagnetic transistor let us talk about a single electromagnetic wave-material computer. Not a big jump in imagining or technological invention maybe. The problem with a silicon transistor or a silicon computer chip is that it cannot move by itself. It needs a human being to carry it from the store to the house, for example. But an electromagnetic computer can be transported easy, without human intervention. The store will broadcast it to your home, just like a radio station or TV station broadcast the signal to your home. But such a transmission is primitive, one way and simple, from sender to receivers.

We need to go one more step for the interesting stuff. Few years ago I had a robot in my home that cleans the floor by itself with no guidance from me. It moves around the room cleaning the floor. Very inexpensive. Robots are very common now in industrial applications and some are available for personal use. A robot is simply a computer that has mechanical parts that can move, such as arms, legs, wheels, propulsion engines, eyes, ears, touch sensors, sonars, etc. If we learn to create mechanical parts made from electromagnetic material, then creating a robot made entirely from non solid state electromagnetic material becomes possible.

This robot when made from electromagnetic material can touch or interact with one human being, or all in a city or a country or earth. The same robot can be extremely small in size and then in an instant change its shape to become extremely large just like a radio or TV signal generated small to instantly enlarge to cover thousands of square or cubic kilometers in size.

By moving from using non solid state EM waves and fields as carriers of information to processing the information in an electromagnetic field, and also the electromagnetic field becoming the structure of the processor or robot, we will have achieved our objective.

Definition of Electromagnetic Field (EMF) Computers: Computers made entirely from electromagnetic fields. They have no electronic or optical or solid state parts, etc. This is a new term I created for a new field in computer design and manufacturing that I thought of.

Definition of Electromagnetic Field Robots: EMF computers that can move controllably in space and have sensors and/or moving parts and forms. This is a new term I created for a new field in robotics design and manufacturing that I thought of.

Random thoughts:

For EMF robotic movement of multiple parts of a single robot, look at schools of fish and birds. Separate physically but can act in unison to appear as one entity. Develop analogous forms in purely electromagnetic moving fields.

Learn to generate shapes and motion from sets of simultaneous math equations. Start with very simple examples and add complexity.

An electric current creates a magnetic field and a magnetic field can create an electric field, and how to twist these fields and mold and intertwine them is what we need to learn to do, to keep the location of this field stationary and under control, and later to create and control functionality and form.

Wireless supply of energy to EM fields: One interesting remote charging tool I came upon by chance was my $200 Diamond Clean Sonic toothbrush (Philips company) that came with a glass drinking cup that also served to charge the tooth brush wirelessly (by using inductive charging), by simply laying the toothbrush inside the cup. Other new such induction energy tools have been invented and are now being brought to market. "Wireless transmission of energy", and an energy field potential in a cup may be used for other purposes in experimentation to constrain the location of EM fields.

Moving from using dispersed light, to laser light (coherent-focused light) dramatically revolutionized what could be invented in highly advanced technological tools and machines. Coherent EM waves use and EM fields may have the same impact on this new EM computer and robotics field.

Currently computer chips and TV screens are made from matrices of millions of transistors. Some use plasma. Can we use these as starting points to make their elements programmable for producing electromagnetic fields. Also to create three dimensional arrays of these matrices to generate interesting electromagnetic fields that will move and do special functions. Eventually, you may learn to create ones that will physically fly from the computer screen as a living robot.

Use random generation and exploration of form and function to meet a specified desired criteria. Can you surround the room by an electromagnetic field for detection, to know when the computer has generated something interesting and can move in space controllably.

Incidentally and an aside. These robots may become somewhat like the spirits I am acquainted with, in terms of form and functionality. But I expect it will be a long time before our robots will acquire their features, but then again, I could be mistaken about the length of development time. But plenty will happen, and the future may carry new interactions, revelations and help that takes humans and their tools far beyond in development. A subject beyond the scope of this booklet at the moment.

(End of Booklet)

Some general random information:

https://en.wikipedia.org/wiki/Maxwell%27s_equations#Maxwell_equations_as_the_classical_limit_of_QED

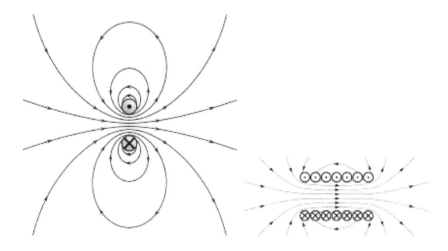

Gauss's law for magnetism: magnetic field lines never begin nor end but form loops or extend to infinity as shown here with the magnetic field due to a ring of current.

Magnetic core memory (1954) is an application of Ampère's law. Each corestores one bit of data.

Maxwell's equations:

Name	Integral equations	Differential equations
Gauss's law	$\oiint_{\partial\Omega} \mathbf{E} \cdot d\mathbf{S} = \dfrac{1}{\varepsilon_0} \iiint_{\Omega} \rho \, dV$	$\nabla \cdot \mathbf{E} = \dfrac{\rho}{\varepsilon_0}$
Gauss's law for magnetism	$\oiint_{\partial\Omega} \mathbf{B} \cdot d\mathbf{S} = 0$	$\nabla \cdot \mathbf{B} = 0$
Maxwell–Faraday equation (Faraday's law of induction)	$\oint_{\partial\Sigma} \mathbf{E} \cdot d\boldsymbol{l} = -\dfrac{d}{dt} \iint_{\Sigma} \mathbf{B} \cdot d\mathbf{S}$	$\nabla \times \mathbf{E} = -\dfrac{\partial \mathbf{B}}{\partial t}$
Ampère's circuital law (with Maxwell's addition)	$\oint_{\partial\Sigma} \mathbf{B} \cdot d\boldsymbol{l} = \mu_0 \left(\iint_{\Sigma} \mathbf{J} \cdot d\mathbf{S} + \varepsilon_0 \dfrac{d}{dt} \iint_{\Sigma} \mathbf{E} \cdot d\mathbf{S} \right)$	$\nabla \times \mathbf{B} = \mu_0 \left(\mathbf{J} + \varepsilon_0 \dfrac{\partial \mathbf{E}}{\partial t} \right)$

In classical electromagnetism, Ampère's circuital law (not to be confused with Ampère's force law that André-Marie Ampère discovered in 1823) relates the integratedmagnetic field around a closed loop to the electric current passing through the loop. James Clerk Maxwell (not Ampère) derived it using hydrodynamics in his 1861 paper "On Physical Lines of Force"[2] and it is now one of the Maxwell equations, which form the basis of classical electromagnetism.

Historic events:

Invention of the transistor

From https://en.wikipedia.org/wiki/History_of_the_transistor:

The first patent[1] for the field-effect transistor principle was filed in Canada by Austrian-Hungarian physicist Julius Edgar Lilienfeld on October 22, 1925, but Lilienfeld published no research articles about his devices, and his work was ignored by industry. In 1934 German physicist Dr. Oskar Heil patented another field-effect transistor. There is no direct evidence that these devices were built, but later work in the 1990s show that one of Lilienfeld's designs worked as described and gave substantial gain…

The Bell Labs work on the transistor emerged from war-time efforts to produce extremely pure germanium "crystal" mixer diodes, used in radar units as a frequency mixerelement in microwave radar receivers. A parallel project on germanium diodes at Purdue University succeeded in producing the good-quality germanium semiconducting crystals that were used at Bell Labs. Early tube-based circuits did not switch fast enough for this role, leading the Bell team to use solid state diodes instead.

The diode

From https://en.wikipedia.org/wiki/Diode:

A diode is a two-terminal electronic component that conducts current primarily in one direction (asymmetric conductance); it has low (ideally zero) resistance in one direction, and high (ideally infinite) resistance in the other. A diode vacuum tube or thermionic diode is a vacuum tube with two electrodes, a heated cathode and a plate, in which electrons can flow in only one direction, from cathode to plate. A semiconductor diode, the most common type today, is a crystalline piece of semiconductor material with a p–n junction connected to two electrical terminals. Semiconductor diodes were the first semiconductor electronic devices. The discovery of asymmetric electrical conduction across the contact between a crystalline mineral and a metal was made by German physicist Ferdinand Braun in 1874. Today, most diodes are made of silicon, but other materials such as gallium arsenide and germanium are used.

Vacuum tube diodes

In 1873, Frederick Guthrie observed that a grounded, white hot metal ball brought in close proximity to an electroscope would discharge a positively charged electroscope, but not a negatively charged electroscope.

In 1880, Thomas Edison observed unidirectional current between heated and unheated elements in a bulb, later called Edison effect, and was granted a patent on application of the phenomenon for use in a dcvoltmeter.

About 20 years later, John Ambrose Fleming (scientific adviser to the Marconi Company and former Edison employee) realized that the Edison effect could be used as a radio detector. Fleming patented the first true thermionic diode, the Fleming valve, in Britain on November 16, 1904 (followed by U.S. Patent 803,684 in November 1905). Throughout the vacuum tube era, valve diodes were used in almost all electronics such as radios, televisions, sound systems and instrumentation. They slowly lost market share beginning in the late 1940s due to selenium rectifier technology and then to semiconductor diodes during the 1960s. Today they are still used in a few high power applications where their ability to withstand transient voltages and their robustness gives them an advantage over semiconductor devices, and in musical instrument and audiophile applications.

On lasers

From https://en.wikipedia.org/wiki/Laser:
In 1917, Albert Einstein established the theoretical foundations for the laser and the maser in the paper Zur Quantentheorie der Strahlung (On the Quantum Theory of Radiation) via a re-derivation of Max Planck's law of radiation, conceptually based upon probability coefficients (Einstein coefficients) for the absorption, spontaneous emission, and stimulated emission of electromagnetic radiation. In 1928, Rudolf W. Ladenburgconfirmed the existence of the phenomena of stimulated emission and negative absorption. In 1939, Valentin A. Fabrikant predicted the use of stimulated emission to amplify "short" waves. In 1947, Willis E. Lamband R.C. Retherford found apparent stimulated emission in hydrogen spectra and effected the first demonstration of stimulated emission. In 1950, Alfred Kastler (Nobel Prize for Physics 1966) proposed the method of optical pumping, experimentally confirmed, two years later, by Brossel, Kastler, and Winter.
Maser
Main article: Maser

Aleksandr Prokhorov
In 1951, Joseph Weber submitted a paper on using stimulated emissions to make a microwave amplifier to the June 1952 Institute of Radio Engineers Vacuum Tube Research Conference at Ottawa, Ontario, Canada. After this presentation, RCA asked Weber to give a seminar on this idea, and Charles Hard Townes asked him for a copy of the paper.
In 1953, Charles Hard Townes and graduate students James P. Gordon and Herbert J. Zeiger produced the first microwave amplifier, a device operating on similar principles to the laser, but amplifying microwave radiation rather than infrared or visible radiation. Townes's maser was incapable of continuous output.[citation needed] Meanwhile, in the Soviet Union, Nikolay Basov and Aleksandr Prokhorov were independently working on the quantum oscillator and solved the problem of continuous-output systems by using more than two energy levels. These gain media could release stimulated emissions between an excited state and a lower excited state, not the ground state, facilitating the maintenance of a population inversion. In 1955, Prokhorov and Basov suggested optical pumping of a multi-level system as a method for obtaining the population inversion, later a main method of laser pumping.
Townes reports that several eminent physicists—among them Niels Bohr, John von Neumann, and Llewellyn Thomas—argued the maser violated Heisenberg's uncertainty principle and hence could not work. Others such as Isidor Rabi and Polykarp Kusch expected that it would be impractical and not worth the effort. In 1964 Charles H. Townes, Nikolay Basov, and Aleksandr Prokhorov shared the Nobel Prize in Physics, "for fundamental work in the field of quantum electronics, which has led to the construction of oscillators and amplifiers based on the maser–laser principle".

Electromagnetic Field

A feedback loop:

The behavior of the electromagnetic field can be divided into four different parts of a loop:
the electric and magnetic fields are generated by electric charges,
the electric and magnetic fields interact with each other,
the electric and magnetic fields produce forces on electric charges,
the electric charges move in space.
A common misunderstanding is that (a) the quanta of the fields act in the same manner as (b) the charged particles that generate the fields. In our everyday world, charged particles, such as electrons, move slowly through matter with a drift velocity of a fraction of a centimeter (or inch) per second, but fields propagate at the speed of light - approximately 300 thousand kilometers (or 186 thousand miles) a second. The mundane speed difference between charged particles and field quanta is on the order of one to a million, more or less. Maxwell's equations relate (a) the presence and movement of charged particles with (b) the generation of fields. Those fields can then affect the force on, and can then move other slowly moving charged particles. Charged particles can move at relativistic speeds nearing field propagation speeds, but, as Einstein showed this requires enormous field energies, which are not present in our everyday experiences with electricity, magnetism, matter, and time and space.
The feedback loop can be summarized in a list, including phenomena belonging to each part of the loop:[citation needed]
charged particles generate electric and magnetic fields
the fields interact with each other
changing electric field acts like a current, generating 'vortex' of magnetic field
Faraday induction: changing magnetic field induces (negative) vortex of electric field
Lenz's law: negative feedback loop between electric and magnetic fields
fields act upon particles
Lorentz force: force due to electromagnetic field
electric force: same direction as electric field
magnetic force: perpendicular both to magnetic field and to velocity of charge
particles move
current is movement of particles
particles generate more electric and magnetic fields; cycle repeats

www.ingramcontent.com/pod-product-compliance
Lightning Source LLC
Chambersburg PA
CBHW080545060326

40690CB00022B/5231